Huey
The Lost Canadian Goose

Adventures on the Trent River

By Debbie MacDonald Taylor

 FriesenPress

Suite 300 - 990 Fort St
Victoria, BC, V8V 3K2
Canada

www.friesenpress.com

ISBN
978-1-5255-3053-1 (Hardcover)
978-1-5255-3054-8 (Paperback)
978-1-5255-3055-5 (eBook)

1. JUVENILE NONFICTION, ANIMALS, DUCKS, GEESE, ETC.

Distributed to the trade by The Ingram Book Company

Thank you to my neighbour Rhonda, who was able to provide a suitable home for Huey; my loving husband, John, who encouraged me to write the story; and my grandchildren, Caelab, Reghan, Kherrington, Averi, MacKinnley, and Nash, who gave me the audience by the fire on the shores of the Trent River.

It was a beautiful, sunny day on Myers Island in the Trent Severn water system. The spring had been unusually rainy and the river was quite high and moving faster than it normally did. We had just left our birthplace and started out on our journey down the Trent River.

My name is Huey, and I was one of eight new goslings. This was our first journey out of our nest.

Like always, my mom and dad were watching all the babies very closely. As we journeyed down the river, I must have gotten distracted by the water's speed. I had slipped away from the others and was all alone.

I swam up and down trying to find my family but they were nowhere in sight.

Suddenly, I saw a rocky shore that I climbed up, and nestled on its side. Just as I was about to fall asleep, I heard a voice. I was curious. It was a sound I had not heard before.

Was that my family? I thought to myself. I let out one peep, and then another, but still no answer.

I saw a little brown dog that was walking around on the grass by the shore, and I, being a curious goose, decided to follow her. She didn't look like anything I had ever seen before. She certainly didn't look like me. She walked on four legs. When I stopped to talk to her, she barked and snorted. I didn't understand her and she didn't understand me.

The little brown dog looked down at me and said, "Why are you here, silly goose? You should be afraid of me. Do you know I am a dog?" I stepped back for a moment, and then continued to follow this animal. We went down the driveway and met up with another white creature. She also walked on four legs. She was also a dog.

So there we were: the little white dog, whose name was Lily; the little brown dog, whose name was Milly; and me.

We walked around and around the yard, sniffing. I don't know what we were sniffing for, but that is what the brown dog and white dog did all day, so I thought I would do the same.

They were trying to understand who I was and I was trying to understand who they were.

When we got tired, White Dog Lily, Brown Dog Milly, and I rested on the nice, deep grass together and enjoyed the warmth of the first nice spring day.

While we were there, a woman and man came out of the house to work on the gardens and they spotted me. I went up to introduce myself and began to follow the lady. She had kind eyes and I knew she would not harm me.

Soon, I was following the brown dog, Milly, and the white dog, Lily, who was following the kind lady, who was following the kind man. We had quite the day walking around the yard watching one another.

It was getting dark and nighttime was approaching. I wondered where I would go. Where would I sleep that night?

The brown dog, the white dog, the woman, and the man would soon go into the house. I was so afraid and alone.

The kind lady came outside to build a nest in the rocks by the river for me. The nest was gentle and soft and it was right on the shore. If my family swam down the river again, I could slip back into the water. They would find me safe and sound.

The morning came, and I noticed the brown dog, Milly, was outside with me. The man came out and so did the lady. I was happy we were all together again.

Maybe the lady could be my mama. The brown and white dogs loved her very much and she was very nice to me. She walked on two legs just like me, not on four like the dogs.

I could pretend she was my mama, so I followed her around and around for another day. Night came again and I slept in my little nest.

The next day was upon us and I didn't see Brown Dog. I slipped into the river and swam a little way until I found another yard. There was another kind lady and another dog, this one a little blonde dog.

The lady's name was Rhonda. She, too, was very kind. Rhonda spoke softly to me and made a safe place for me out of the rain. She brought me some food. I was so happy with Rhonda and her little dog. Ena introduced herself to me and we became friends. Rhonda and Ena made me feel safe.

I followed Rhonda wherever she went. When she cut the grass, I followed behind her and was able to eat all the freshly cut grass I wanted. Ena and I would chase one another around and around in and out of the river. We had so much fun! At nighttime, I would go to sleep in a dog house.

I was growing big and I noticed other geese on the river, flying and landing. But they were not like me. My wings were different. Rhonda called them "angel wings." As hard as I tried, I could not fly.

That made me very sad. How was I to find my family if I could not fly?

Rhonda loved to canoe and she asked if I would like to journey down the river with her and Ena. Ena the blonde dog would sit in the canoe and I would follow them, as I was a good swimmer. It was so peaceful floating down the river with them. I saw White Dog Lily and Brown Dog Milly. We stopped by the dock to visit for a while, and then finished our journey.

Other geese would stop by to play with me. After our playtime, I would go back to be with Rhonda and Ena.

One day, Rhonda took me for a truck ride to a school. We went to visit her grade one and two class. Those children were funny. They walked on two legs, just like me! They loved to feed me and it was such a fun day.

Rhonda's friends at the school said she should take me to a sanctuary. They felt that Canadian Geese should not be pets. I had never been to a sanctuary. I was not sure what to expect.

We met the people at the sanctuary, and they were all very nice. But Rhonda could not part with me. She said I was family now. We journeyed back home in the truck to see Ena and my other friends.

I was a different goose. I looked different from the other geese on the river. I had funny wings that stuck out and I was unable to fly, like my friends. I certainly was a different goose. But I learned that being different did not mean no one would love you. Being different did not mean you could never have a family.

I am so happy to be part of Rhonda's family. We lie in the grass together. We sit on the dock and watch the other geese. We cut the lawn together. We canoe down the river, and run in circles. I still visit with White Dog Lily and Brown Dog Milly. I swim down the river to be with them and the lady walks me home on the road at dark. She keeps me safe. All the neighbours on Myers Island love me and I have a wonderful home.

I have learned a family does not need to look like you or act like you. If they love you, you can be a family.

I may not be able to fly like all the others, but I live and stay on the Trent River with my new family. I swim with the other geese during the day and sleep on the shore of the river in a dog house at night.

It sometimes is special to be a little different!

Notes:

Huey still lives with Rhonda and Ena by the river. He has a heated dog house and a pen to keep him safe.

Canadian Geese can live between ten and twenty-four years. They eat grass, and like to sleep in the water or near the water to protect them from predators. When a goose finds a mate, they stay with them for life.

Lily and Milly also live on Myers Island, just south of Campbellford, Ontario, and are still friends with Huey.

Rhonda says Huey understands words, and comes when he is called.

CPSIA information can be obtained
at www.ICGtesting.com
Printed in the USA
LVHW071905030219
606243LV00001B/2/P